Promises of Poison

Victoria Lauren

DEDICATION

Here's to the ones who dream, foolish as they may seem.

Here's to the hearts that ache.

Here's to the mess we make.

Ice Queen

Once upon a time

There was a very angry girl

And this very angry girl

Lived in a very angry world.

One where cupboard doors were always slammed

And doors rattled on their hinges.

You could hear her by her stomps

And she never smiled with her eyes.

This little girl was powered by poison and lightning

Bottled up inside

Until one day she very nearly died of it.

One small girl cannot carry that much anger within her

Without being boiled alive.

She ate snow handful by handful,

The soft cold nothingness coating her throat,

Snowflakes scattered across her face.

Each icy mouthful slowly soothing the fire in her belly.

And slowly so slowly it seemed as though it would never work,

The girl learned the love the snow

As much as she loves the fire.

CATARACTS

Van Gogh cut his ear off

Placed it in a box lined with satin

And gave it to his love.

There's something about cutting off part of yourself

Offering it on a silver platter while the blood still drips

That makes so much sense to me.

Or maybe he thought he could cut off part of him

And the love would seep out with the blood.

Maybe he wanted to get rid of it.

Maybe he had too much.

Maybe it was poisoning him from the inside out.

That is a feeling I know well.

Weed Killer

Love is a choice.

It might sprout

Like a green stem between sidewalk cracks

Concrete crumbled just enough

To take root.

It's a good thing I'm a gardener.

It's a good thing I can pull weeds.

Because it's too easy for me to love.

And I love so hard.

HEMICERATOIDES HIEROGLYPHICA

There is a moth

In the lands of Madagascar

Called hemigraoides hieroglyhphica

That drinks tears in the middle of the night to stay alive.

Sometimes I think you must do the same with me,

That you make me cry on purpose.

That it sustains you somehow.

Debt Collectors

You taught me there was a debt I must pay

By being a pretty little girl

Good little girl

Silly little girl

Quiet little girl.

Then I became

Mad little girl

Sad little girl

Out-of-her-mind little girl

Who grew up to be

Soft little girl

Vicious little girl

Strong little girl.

Desolate Days

When my grandma had a heart attack

I went into the bathroom and tore out all my eyelashes.

Plucked out all of them with my fingers.

A sharp *yank, tug, pop!*

Let them flutter to the floor.

One after another after another after another.

They were too beautiful.

This was not a time for beauty.

LOVESICK

Lovesick

They whisper in the streets.

The girl is lovesick.

So maybe I am.

Maybe I stuff myself with milk and honey until it's running in rivulets

down my chin.

Maybe I twirl in the forest just because I am drunk on the feeling of the

wind on my face.

Maybe I whisper to the moon and wish upon stars,

Stuffing my pockets full of lovely moment after lovely moment after lovely

moment after.

Maybe I'm lovesick.

Maybe I'm feverish with my own desire.

Whistles in the Night

Nice girls don't have fangs.

Nice girls don't kiss and tell.

Nice girls don't speak to people that way.

Nice girls don't paint their nails with venom.

Nice girls don't use blood for lipstick,

Hiding razor blades behind their teeth.

Nice girls smile

And say thank you

When someone has them by the neck.

Nice girls walk around without anger brewing in their chests,

Without acid in their throats,

And don't scream at the sky.

Nice girls don't cry

Don't fight against the panic and hysteria welling inside their stomachs.

Nice girls aren't overcome with terror when a noise happens nearby.

Maybe I was never a nice girl at all.

Nice girls don't scream.

Eye of the Beholder

People used to commission tiny portraits of their lovers' eyes.

The eye of their lover minute, handheld,

Mysteriously vague but oh-so-telling.

You were loved.

They kept the photos locked around their necks,

At the base of their throats

Next to their pulses.

That's where I'll keep you,

Close enough to choke me.

CANDY-COATED-MISERY

I hate Thanksgiving.

The stuffing I can handle.

Being trapped in a room full of barely restrained hands, I cannot

Forks poised over plates and throats at the same time

Spitting candy-coated-vitriol over the tops of the good china always stirs my

stomach.

Hotel Swimming Pool

There's something about that echoey humid room,

An empty swirling hot tub,

Too much glass.

And I lay here in the middle of a pool,

All alone

Yet not alone at all.

Any minute another guest could join me,

Force me from my solitude,

Intrude.

I lay here in the middle of a large pool,

My hair gently swirling out from my skull,

And I stare.

Counting the ceiling tiles.

Breathe in.

Breathe out.

Breathe in.

Breathe out.

So, this is healing.

Soft Hands Part I

Years ago, I decided the allow myself to love soft things.

Eventually

I too, became something soft.

I let myself return to loving.

Fairytale Girl

Briars tangled in my curls,

Dirt smeared across my cheekbones,

Fingernails bloody and raw,

I crawled out from between the thicket of leaves.

I love with sharp teeth.

All blood and scratches

Behind my kisses.

Fairy tale dust still clings to my skin,

My eyes sleep stained,

Lipstick smeared from true love's kiss.

I am awake again.

Cut Scene

It's about the tiniest things in the end.

The way your lips pursed when I laughed too loud at dinner.

The way your eyes flitted about to see if anyone saw us.

How your hand hesitated before taking mine.

All of that said more than you did.

Carousel Music

I read in old books about how there used to be brass rings hidden among the
ceilings of carousel rides.

What a romantic notion.

Right place,

Right time.

You can grab the ring and pull.

The lights would flash, and bells would ring,

And you would win a prize.

Maybe that's part of my reason my romantic little self is always looking up-

Trying to spy the brass ring of life.

Diet of a Growing Girl

I sink my teeth into Barbie doll legs like a drumstick.

Chomp Polly pockets rubbery head off.

Lick satin bows clean from my fingers.

Shovel piles of glitter into my mouth.

I stuff myself.

Gorge myself on the little bits and bobs of lace and femininity.

I drink gallons of Pepto-pink paint.

Sip sunsets the shade of bubblegum.

Chug the silvery glowingness of moonlight

And polish it all off with an aperitif of silk nighties.

When I need a snack, I chew tacks,

Swallow nails,

And pluck screws from the walls before popping them into my mouth.

All of this helps me grow into the woman I am.

Mothers Wisdom

Every spring my mother dreams of mushrooms.

Dreams of them sprouting on the forest floor

And she wakes in a fever.

Following their whispers,

She disappears into the woods.

Following her roots,

She wanders,

Eyes glued to the forest floor.

Searching.

I watch her go over the hills

In search of mushrooms,

In search of childhood memories,

In search of herself.

Fᴀʟʟ Rɪsᴋ

And so on the nights my aching lungs heave

Not wanting to take a single more breath,

Not wanting to face another dreadful morning mist

Eyes gummy and thick,

Hot from tears,

Throbbing temples,

Hair tangled into nests to store my sadness as it multiplies and births a new

generation,

Remember-

There will always be that moment

That sunshine hazy

Butter mellow moment

Where you think quietly

"God I'm so glad I stuck it out

I'm so glad I stayed."

And so, I choose to inhale again.

Over and over

Breathing through the pain slicing me into pieces.

Destroying me from the inside out.

Nicotine Addiction

My fingers itch for the cigarette I've never allowed myself to have.

Knowing the twitching hands attached to me would love it just a bit too

much,

Would crave it just a bit too often.

I daydream of taking deep puffs

Feeling the stress melting off my shoulders.

At cheap souvenir shops, I look at the ashtrays,

Glittery and plastic

And think of what it's like to fill them with full of ashes.

I flick the idea from my mind

Picturing my already asthmatic lungs stuffed with black tar ready to burst.

I think about the glowing embers lighting the inky night.

I think of my fingertips yellowed and worn.

The satisfying sound a pack makes as you smack it on the counter.

I think of the red glow it would cast against my face as I inhaled the smoke

deeper still

Choking on it

The curl of smoke in my throat

Loving the way my hands look holding the slim paper.

I know all this.

And it's why I've never allowed a cigarette in these hands.

Victorian Floral Language

So speak to me in the language of flowers

Whispers and secret meanings lost from times gone by

Messages and codes riddles among the petals.

You and I both see the words

Dancing between the bouquets.

PURSE SWEETS

I hand out compliments like candy

Because when I kept them

They rotted my teeth and ate away my brain.

Fever

There's something that comes over me in the dead of winter

When the snow is pushed up against the house tight.

I catch a fever.

Sweating bullets in the single digits

I throw open all the windows.

While I sleep the snow comes inside the house

Piling up on the windowsills

Tucking itself into bed with me.

It finally cools my brow.

Tucked between the sheets against my bare hot dry skin

Something in me melts away.

Until finally this fever I shake

Right when the snow melts under the warm hands on the sun again.

Recycling Program

So I sit with my stomach full of bullets and slowly I spit them back up.

Softly landing in my hands,

Not pointed at anyone anymore.

Not even myself.

This anger

I'm slowly regurgitating,

This hatred

I no longer abuse myself with.

Letting each bullet I choke and cough out

Leave my system for good.

Telling myself that anger isn't needed anymore to keep me safe.

Knitting Club

There are spiders under my skin.

There they are

Weaving and bobbing and itching and throbbing and

There they go again

Legs skating beneath the surface

Scratching

Never catching

My skin shifts above their rotund bodies

Lumps moving

Roiling just beneath my touch

I see their legs knitting what must be pieces of me back together

Fixing me as fast as they're able with needle legs

The wriggling bulbous mounds heaving across my body

Skin grotesquely rippling above

As the spiders spin and knit me back together again.

GREEN LIGHTS

That's the best thing a girl can be in this world,

A beautiful little fool,

Right?

And god,

I was,

The fool I was.

Sometimes I want to go back and shake her.

Hold her by the shoulders and heave to and fro

Rip the hair out from the roots

Drag the smile from her lips.

Sometimes I want to hold her hand,

Cry,

Hold her tight.

Tell her it will get worse

But it will also get better

And I'm sorry.

I wish I could tell that girl I'm so sorry.

For not believing in her

For closing her into a box

For not being kinder and gentler and more loving.

I was a beautiful little fool

I am a beautiful little fool.

New Leands

The first time I took an international flight it was nine hours overnight.

I sat by the window and couldn't sleep a wink.

I jangled like a person needing their fix,

Tension and anxiety and excitement wrapped into one turbulent emotion.

The first night I spent in your arms I did the same thing.

Was too in awe

Couldn't close my eyes

Couldn't rest

I had to take it all in

Awake without dreaming

As your chest rose and fell behind me

I knew when the sun rose again on the new day, I would be in a new land

Unlike any other I had ever known.

Fangs

You know why I am so intrigued with the idea of vampires?

Why I desperately wish they could be real?

Because I know that in my glitter tights and velvet headband and satin dress

Walking with my friends in the dark of night it would be

This power

To just be in the moment.

Giggling, tipsy, enjoying the stars,

Dressed to the nines,

Drunk on the magic of it all.

Walking under the moonlight,

Lazily strolling down a cobblestone road,

Holding hands.

That's how I want it to go.

To know there's no danger if I am the danger.

Ballet of Not Caring:

Act Three

Scene Two

So, we are keeping secrets again.

I notice it,

You don't.

I'm polite.

I nod.

I smile.

I watch.

You aren't telling the truth again.

New Home Smell

The scent of someone else on my skin used to sicken me.

I would fidget and itch,

Wanting to rip the skin from my bones,

Burn the clothes I wore.

Gagging on the unfamiliar

Poison on the back of my throat.

But with you-

With you, it doesn't turn my stomach.

With you, it just smells like home.

TAMED

I am my mother's savage daughter,

But my mother forgot how to be.

It was like watching a strong lioness

Beaten into a house cat.

Two Sisters and the Moon

I used to be a nanny

A long time ago

And I watched two little girls,

Two tiny sisters,

And the smallest one

Used to stare up at the moon,

With a love and a hunger in her eyes.

She would beg

For me to get her the moon.

To bring it down

And hand it over

So she could hold it between her palms.

I would watch her jump,

Fingers arching up,

Trying to catch the moon from her place in the sky.

I tried telling her that wasn't how it worked-

The moon was up there-

And we were down here-

There was too much space between.

She simply didn't believe me.

Or maybe she didn't care.

Or maybe she just believed in herself more than simple words could assuage.

And I watched that girl jump and arch and strain,

Wishing her way to the moon.

Eyes Full of Reverence

You kneel at my feet,

Prostrating in penance

All my holiness in plain view.

I radiate across the room.

I am holy.

I am holy.

I am holy.

The key to your salvation

There is truth on my tongue.

Mecca.

Woman.

Goddess.

Deity divine.

You kneel,

Fervent,

Prayerful,

Pleas for heaven on your lips.

I Had a Big Lunch

Empty used to be the only feeling I felt good with.

Empty

Empty

Empty

Empty is clean.

Empty is good.

Empty is strong.

Food is gross.

Food is bad.

Food is sin.

Empty is strong, pure, and lovely.

Full is bad, bad, bad.

And I am a good good girl.

I don't eat but my waist doesn't shrink.

I get dizzy dizzy dizzy

Suck it up buttercup.

Beautiful girls are small girls.

Small girls are worthy girls.

Worthy girls are loved girls.

And don't you finally want to be loved?

Don't you want to be pretty?

Don't you want to be good?

Because if big is bad then I'm the worst.

Empty means smaller and smaller means better

Right right right?

Isn't that right,

Good good girl?

Good job

Skipping lunch.

Good job

Only eating what you must.

Good job

Being strong strong strong.

You just need to be a little stronger

And get smaller

To get smarter

To get superior.

To eat you have to earn it,

And to earn it you have to push push push.

Push past tired

Push past hungry

Push past to clear.

Clear is empty and empty is good

Uh oh.

What was that?

You broke.

You weren't even that hungry we're you?

Now you feel icky, don't you?

That horrible feeling of food in your stomach

Ugh

Don't you worry,

Tomorrow you'll be stronger.

Tomorrow you'll be prettier.

Tomorrow you'll be braver.

Tomorrow you'll be empty.

Ice Picks

If you had the chance,

 I know

You would drive an ice pick through my eye socket

 And take out everything that makes me who I am.

Try and reset me

To a blank canvas,

Remake me,

Under your hands.

Birthright

Sometimes being a woman feels like nothing but a curse.

These hands made for carrying emotional burdens and scraping together

excuses and stitching together all that is broken.

Lips made for soft demure smiles and sucking and licking.

Hips made for unwanted touches and birthing and bruises from doorways.

Sometimes I feel as though my body does not belong to me,

That I am the last one deserving of her.

That it is only a matter of time before I am touched yet again by someone I

do not want touching me.

That as a woman this is just a quiet yet expected chore.

That I owe them something-

A show

A touch

A smile.

Sometimes I feel like everything has been taken from me and nothing was given.

LABYRINTH

I have cut my fingertips open

And drawn a map through my heart for you.

Ripped my hair out and braided you an escape ladder.

Given you every single thing and more I could think of to get you to stay,

And then watched while you left.

Soft Hands Part II

I've never laid my hands on someone without love flowing out of my fingertips.

Why then do I assume people touch me with revulsion?

WINTER COATS IN SPRING

I do not flinch when you move quickly

Because I have never seen you do anything hurtful with your hands.

I do not tremble when you raise your voice

Because it has never been raised in anger at me.

Slowly, Imperceptibly,

I'm trusting you

More and more.

Enough to start shedding the layers that kept me safe before.

Ballet Slippers

I wish I was a ballerina.

That I could throw my body into geometric breathing,

Screaming without a sound,

Aching aching aching

Every arch of the arm a masterpiece,

Every twirl a study in patience.

I kept only the slippers,

None of the art.

A Thousand Times Goodnight

Sweet dreams is the kindest, most lovely thing you can say to someone.

"Sweet dreams," you say,

Your words tucking them into bed.

Keeping watch through the night,

Making sure only the beautiful and loving dreams get in.

"Sweet dreams," you whisper,

Cloaking them in an incantation full of mercy, of love.

"Sweet dreams," you breathe,

Laying the words across their shoulders like a warm blanket.

Tucking wishes into their pockets for later like sweets,

For them to melt sweet dreams on the backs of their tongues.

Permission Slip

You bump up against every safety net I've installed

To keep myself from falling too deep.

The alarms go off,

Shrill and sharp,

But still I keep going.

You could break me,

But I'll let you,

Simply because I trust you not to.

Field Amputation

I don't want to sit in the trenches with you anymore.

I had to leave

Because my shoes were full of mud and my lips were full of bullet holes

And I deserved to see the sunshine for a change.

I didn't want to sit in the trenches with you anymore

Because I couldn't handle dragging myself and you through it all.

Dodging gunfire,

Inhaling too much smoke,

My hands full of glass shattered like all the promises you made to change,

Like all the promises you made to try.

It was only me.

Only my two arms, only my brute force,

Getting us through the minefield

And I couldn't do it anymore.

Signature Color

My lips curl around my straw and when I take them away

It is stained

Blood red

Like everything else I've ever touched.

PROMISES OF POISON

Promises of poison on my lips

I whisper honeyed lies into your ear.

Posed and poised as ever to begin.

Whatever it takes to get you to leave.

Whatever it takes to get you to stay.

Another Life, Perhaps?

I notice every single funeral home I pass.

I wish I was inside

Helping stitch on people's smiles.

Not just the deceased

But of those left behind.

Piggy Banks

Whenever something horrible happens to me—

We are talking something that makes me want to lie down

And never get back up again—

Something that makes me want to climb up on a stool

Something that makes me walk to the edges of ledges and calculate the drop

below—

Something that shatters me,

Mind, body, and spirit.

I scrape together whatever money I have.

Nickels and dimes clanging together from change jars,

Bank account totally drained,

Piggy bank smashed to bits,

Credit card in hand,

And I get on an airplane.

I go as far away as I can afford to try and find myself again.

Sometimes it's my own backyard and sometimes I can run as far as the sun

can reach.

And I go forward.

I find somewhere new

For the wind to whip my hair out of my face,

And yank my dress,

And I hike across cobblestones,

And city blocks,

And mountain trails,

Until I feel the breath breathe back into me.

Until my Sepia turns back into color.

Until my heart feels less shattered.

I look at you.

I look deep into your eyes,

And I start saving my dollars in jars again,

Because you are everything that could shatter me

Far across the sea.

Hugstained

Oh, we loved each other so well,

You and I.

We did.

We truly lived and loved well.

You in your sweaters,

And I in my dresses.

Both of us wandering through the tough terrain together,

Tripping along the route,

Making a joyful noise as we went along.

Love is wearing down my edges,

Making me faded and touched and hugstained.

SUNGLASSES

One day

I'll look at love with the sun shining from my eyes

And I won't flinch

When it looks back.

GREY SPACE

My friend Britt is a 911 operator.

She works in the middle of the night,

When things seem to go wrong.

I think of her steady and capable voice,

Strong and ready for emergencies,

Guiding people through their late-night panics.

I think of what it's like to be able to pick up the phone and be told it will all

be okay.

It will all be handled.

Help is on the way.

But my house isn't on fire

And there's no one at my door.

I wish I could call and have her sweet strong tones guide me through

 Until the grey light spills in my window for morning.

Nerve Endings

Singing is magic.

Something you can't hold with your hands.

Something deep within.

It stimulates your vagus nerve

Which slows down your heart rate,

Lowers your blood pressure,

Calms you down.

I wonder if that's why I never shut up as a child,

Incessantly humming,

Singing until my voice was broken.

Louder and higher and stronger until I was breathless.

Until I felt like I was drowning without the water.

It was the only thing I could do.

Night Terrors

My back teeth ache.

My skin flayed open, neck to sternum

Exposing my tendons,

My wrists swimming in blood.

Grasping hands wishing for another to hold.

Wishing I wasn't alone,

Spluttering into the darkness.

The moon looks so big

And I am so small, bleeding out beneath her.

Jolted awake with the sound of the nightmares still ringing in my ears,

Lungs full of water,

Eyes rubbed red,

Feeling utterly disjointed

Like I can't get my body to move the way it usually does.

It's here again.

Nightmares are having something to lose.

Being A Woman at a Coffee Shop

Be careful, she whispers, haunted eyes staring at mine

You too, I murmur back with a hunted glance

Our hands brushed as you handed me my latte.

Hoarder House

Your skin smells sour.

The milk's gone bad.

There's mold all over.

And I'm so sad.

Good Mourning

I think about Victorian Tear Catchers quite a bit.

The fact that widows would cry directly into them,

Bottling their tears in crystal vials decorated with golden crosses,

And when it was full

And all their tears evaporated away to become part of something else.

They too were told they were allowed to stop grieving,

To move on.

I will never move on from you.

I will carry my tear vial always.

A Rose by Any Other Name

In Ancient Rome, roses represented secrecy and delicacy and discreetness.

Maybe that's why I drag so many into my home—

To keep quiet—

To keep sweet.

Now I Take Lexapro

When I was a little girl and I had to cut something for classwork art

I would stress so hard

And tell myself to give up before scissors even touched paper

Because even when I tried my hardest it was still not good enough.

As a teen, if I had to cut something out

I would beg my mother to do it for me.

For her strokes were sure and straight

And mine wobbled

No matter how long I took to check the lines.

As an adult I just make sure never to cut.

BLIZZARD

I hope we get snowed in.

Close up all the doorways

White out the rest of the world

Soften all the edges.

I want to be here with you.

The rest of it erased for just a little while.

Everything quiet.

Nothing else but this.

PYREX AND ARSENIC

I was raised to focus on caregiving.

Told the best thing I could be was a kind provider

To cook and clean

And if I was smart?

Well, what a lovely addition.

So, I took my apron

And my spatula

And I burned the house to the ground.

PREMONITIONS

My teacher looked at me once

After I tearfully admitted that I felt like a failure looking at my test results

And she looked at me,

Eyes burning,

Angry,

Shining with rage,

And quietly grasped my hand,

Whispering fiercely

"Never say that out loud ever again.

It makes it true."

Emeralds and Butterflies

There's a story from long ago,

That a woman had to watch the one she loved die.

She cried so hard her tears turned into emeralds

And screamed so deeply butterflies came out her throat

She was devastated.

Now whenever I'm at my lowest,

I check for sparkles in my bile,

Hoping for something to come out of all the heartbreak.

Fair Verona Boy

There's something about you that makes me ask you to swear not on the

moon

The inconstant moon

Actually, if we are being honest,

To not swear at all.

I daydream of your laugh, as thou art thyself

You make me want to play the ingenue

When I kept casting myself as the evil stepmother my whole life long.

Take all myself.

To hug you goodbye thinking parting is such sweet sorrow.

For the first time unafraid

Knowing you are steady,

You are kind.

Like a tree in a storm

You will calmly look at me the same way,

Full of love.

So I shall say goodnight till it be morrow.

Hit Snooze

When you spend enough time being terrified

Eventually your racing heart becomes the thrum that rocks you to sleep

And the panic alarm is the funky beat you dance to in your mirror.

It makes sense how you slipped in.

I was already used to all the screaming.

Drake Passage

I would sign up for a cruise to the Antarctic with you.

Would don my mittens and wrap myself head to toe in soft, warm textiles,

Get in a huge grey steel ship,

Sail off into the darkness with you.

Sleep on rollicking beds inside the belly of the sea,

Look from portholes at the vast nothingness that can be the sea in her fugue
state,

And finally wash upon another shore
With your hand in mine.

We would walk across the snow,

Look for penguins,

Watch the ice floes moving and breathing and creaking and chattering

amongst themselves.

I want to write you love letters at sea and mail them home so they stack up

for you on our doorstep.

Bottle ocean water for you to wash your hair in.

Buy your favorite snacks ready to whip out the second I notice you're having

a sad day.

I want to learn to knit to make sweaters to keep you warm

And then tuck you into my arms at night,

Pulling you close,

Our breathing the only sound other than the waves.

I'll go with you anywhere.

Haven't I Seen This Wallpaper?

There are times I fear I'm nothing but a madwoman in the wallpaper.

Haunting this old house that is my body,

Creaks and aches come with the territory.

I'm the terror living in these walls.

There are other women here

And we dance

In the sickly yellow light.

I'm nothing more than a haunted house.

Seedlings

Haven't gone to church in years

But at times I catch myself praying

I'm not exactly sure to who.

God, Allah, myself, Jesus, the universe, a white light, love itself, the moon,

maybe my mom,

Whoever is listening,

Thank you.

I catch myself throwing out wishes and hopes and dreams

Like dandelion fluff catching the wind.

I don't know where it ends up.

I just know it's beautiful.

Like seeds taking root somewhere new.

Wishes scattered across the lands.

DRIPPING

There are days I feel I do nothing but ache and leak.

Leak milk.

Leak blood.

Leak tears.

Everything leaks.

Pouring forth from me

Until I'm wrung dry.

Is this all I'm good for?

Cold Girl

Too much sun makes me nervous.

Spooks me to the core.

I long for dark and dreary days.

Wind biting my nose,

Chapping my hands,

Clawing at the scarf around my neck.

Cut down to the core of me,

Slice me to my ribs,

Steal the breath from my lungs,

Whip my hair into knots.

Just don't shine in my face.

Please don't send me sunny skies.

Like a vampire,

They send me to mourning.

Packing my bags,

Chasing the dark.

Too much sun makes me nervous.

I long for snow drifts,

Storm clouds and freezing temperatures,

Black ice and squalling skies.

While some flourish under the warm rays

I wilt.

Wilt and wilt until I'm brown and dead.

My soul long past suffering.

No,

I need clouded skies

Where the dirt is too cold and packed to dig.

I see what the sun does for you.

Revitalizes you.

Refreshes you.

Softens you.

Kisses your skin.

Brightens your hair.

It depletes me.

It sucks me dry.

The sun bakes the last will I had out.

I feel it evaporating again.

I wait for the snow.

GIRLHOOD

Right away we learn to stick to the back of the house

When that certain weird guy comes in

With a hungry look in his eyes.

To lie

When people call and ask for other girls by name,

Ignore when they claim to be her uncle, her dad, her friend, her brother.

Act like we didn't want to wear our hair in a grabbable ponytail,

To park under streetlamps,

Walk out with the touchy-but-ultimately-harmless work guy at the end of

the night.

We learn to make concessions.

To make amends.

To make sacrifices.

To make choices.

That our body isn't always ours.

Neither is our time.

That our words have been laid claim to already

By someone else's voice.

Pocket Full of Sunshine

My memories fade so quickly lately.

I wish I could tuck them all away

Into the pockets of my winter coats

And pull them out when I come across them again

Ghosts of smog and smoke and sea spray wafting off of them still

Worn around the edges from passing my fingers over them too many times

Trying to keep the memories with me.

Well Actually Frankenstein Was the Scientist

I am Frankenstein girl,

Stitched together

With pieces of the people I know.

Ripping the grace from one

Stitched into my trauma.

Wrenching the humor from my old best friend

Laying it over my cracks in my heart like fondant,

The sugar eats away everything else.

Stole the righteous anger

From a girl in a coffee shop who I watched throw her drink into his face.

I paste it with craft glue on top of my ripped self-esteem.

Constantly tearing out the rotting pieces of myself,

Black market new models inserted, stitching myself closed.

Healing and ripping and bleeding and sobbing and peeling and screaming.

I am Frankenstein girl.

Now I Take Ambien

There's something about knowing that just seventy years ago

I would have been covered in white cotton,

Locked away in a room,

Awaiting a date with an ice pick through the eye socket

For feeling my desolate little feelings.

I think about it whenever I can't sleep.

Highway Mile Markers

There's a time when you have been driving for a while

Where the darkness has pressed so hard on all the sides of your car

That you feel like less of a traveler

And more like what it must feel like to be all alone.

The last person on earth

Where the thrum of the tires

And the ache in your chest match rhythms.

Help Desk

I no longer suffer quietly.

I allow my pain

To cry out.

I no longer tear my fingertips open

Scraping scraggly surfaces for purchase,

Feeling the blood pour forth,

Ripping fingernails off.

Bone protruding from torn skin

With my lips pursed shut.

Now I gnash my teeth.

Let the tears pour forth,

Saltwater cleansing and scalding my skin.

I howl.

Shriek for help,

Screaming my throat sore.

I reach my hands out

 Grasping others to me.

Please help me.

Please don't make me do this alone.

Dusk

Maybe that's how they'll remember me.

Romantic dresses,

Dim candlelight,

A small smile on my face.

Glamorous rooms full of love.

Flowers strewn in my hair,

Nails lacquered red and sharp,

Lips flashing the color of blood.

I hope you remember how I flicker like a candle in the dark.

Boundaries

I'm always covered in bruises.

My pale skin covered in dark splotches,

Butterfly kisses from pain

I'm constantly running into things.

Bumping them,

Being jostled,

Forgetting where the boundaries are.

It's good to have reminders.

These blossoms of pain on my skin

Dyed deep deep dark

On my pale pale skin

Reminding me that I'm breakable.

Reminding me there are rules.

Reminding me you get hurt when you get too close.

What is it that's so feminine to me about bruises?

Is it the way pain translates into a bloom on the skin?

The fact we carry the traumas on us?

The way we start out unmarred and end up marked?

Skin's delicate and forgetful memory.

Lighthouse Keepers

If I could have what I wanted

Anything

Everything

It would be foggy cool mornings

In a house by the sea.

Afternoons in our sunroom

Underneath a rainstorm,

Book in my lap,

Tea at my elbow.

Evenings by the fire

Holding your hand in mine.

A house so full of love

It shines bright out the windows

Guiding all the ships home.

Dreams of Fairy Hills

So I tuck myself into white satin,

Brush my hair back,

Cover myself in rose-scented tonics.

Flick on the nightlight so the shadows can't find me.

Rest my head on silk pillowcases

And dream of fairy tales until the harsh light of morning comes again.

Foggy Glasses

Sometimes I worry that you see me

Wrong.

Rose colored glasses or too much hope clouding your eyes.

That you see me

Slanted,

Crooked,

Through your heart.

Feral Cat

Family doesn't look good on me.

It doesn't look easy.

It doesn't fit natural.

My skin is stretched too tight around my body,

And my lips are pulled too thin around my mouth,

And my elbows stick out too much for easy hugging,

And my voice is too sharp for play.

Family doesn't look good on me.

It doesn't come easily.

I'm not used to being accountable to someone.

Sometimes I'm angry.

Sometimes I feel caged.

Sometimes I miss airplanes.

But it doesn't mean I want to leave.

I'm just not used to being here.

I'm used to being alone.

But you keep me anyhow.

Thank goodness.

What's New

The plant by the front door is dying.

Browning and drying and drifting away.

I feel myself doing the same,

Crumbling to bits with the breeze.

I can't find it in me to care about either.

Hot Air Balloon Kisses

It was never a problem when I floated away from the earth

Because you sent me balloons every morning.

Pink, heart-shaped mylar

So I knew you were thinking of me.

Sometimes they had love letters tied to their strings.

And on the days you really missed me

You took a hot air balloon up just to kiss my lips and stroke my hair

To have a giggle together

Before you headed back down

Feet again on the ground.

And I sent you presents too.

Flowers dropping into your lap,

Rain for your flowers on particularly dry days,

And once my heart was full of enough sunshine again,

I would send you myself.

Do You See Me?

Simmering underneath every single conversation with my mother is that 14-year-old girl full to the brim of anger

Why don't you love me the ways I need to be loved

Every conversation silently screams

Why do I repulse you

Boils under every smile

Every unspoken word hangs thick in the air between us.

Weeds

Pick up the ax and lop off the hand

Trimming it back like a tree

Pruning down to the root of me whenever I start to grow back.

That giving hand of mine that reaches out,

That sweet spirit that goes to other people,

Nothing but dangerous in these times,

Proven again and again.

I see new growth.

Gritting my teeth

Rolling my neck

Coiling my biceps

I lop my fingers off once again.

Nothing safe about kindness here.

Maybe one day the weakness will stop growing back.

CRAVINGS

Most of my year is spent missing the hiss of autumn.

The crunch of crispy grass under boots

And the heavy wet leaves piled on top of each other.

I miss the oranges and purples and reds exploding like fireworks before they

give way to snowstorms again.

They Were Cheaper

For weeks after I stunk like calla lilies.

Their scent somehow stuck to my skin.

I scrubbed and scrubbed.

You knew I loved spray roses,

But somehow all my hands ever held

Were calla lilies.

Flowers are flowers in your eyes.

Projectile Vomiter

I don't have the stomach for life.

My stomach churns

I gag on my days

Choke down the hours.

Puke up my failures

Retch on my responsibilities

When I get attached to someone, my heart doesn't glow-

Bile bites the back of my throat

Constricting my airways.

I gasp.

Desperate for less.

A stronger constitution.

A tougher stomach.

Motherhood

When I first saw you, I was sitting at the dining table

And I thought my nerves were for the tall boy making me dinner.

Then I saw your bright blue eyes,

Your long blonde hair,

And you looked right at me.

That's when I knew:

I was in trouble.

I knew in that moment I would love you.

I knew in that moment I would keep you.

I knew in that moment you were my baby.

Call it a mother's intuition.

Call it fate.

But now I call you to dinner.

Stroke your hair,

Kiss the top of your head,

And tuck you to bed.

Like I knew I would

From the second I met you.

I knew I was in trouble because this was everything I had ever wanted.

Even tried to leave a few times,

Overwhelmed,

Undeserving,

Shocked he was handing it to me on a silver platter with a kiss.

A family.

Now I watch both my boys sleep at night

Their hair wild and splayed across pillows,

Snoring and talking and moving always.

Both the loves of my life.

I'm the luckiest girl in the world.

Sea Sirens

When I say I have a love for mermaids

I don't mean the gorgeous ones with swirling red hair.

I mean the translucent-skinned girls from the deep

Whose voices lure men deeper offshore

Whose skin is as black as the night they call from

Whose teeth are as sharp as their wit

Whose fear is buried in treasure chests deep below the sea.

The girls who tamed the sea and the shore

Who hunt men more vicious than nightmares.

Tarnished Necklaces

Years and years I spent with a cross around my throat,

Thorns in my tongue,

Rose petals on my palm,

Holy water pouring from my eyes.

I did it all.

Inked symbols into my skin,

Prayed again and again,

Begged for salvation,

To be saved.

One day I realized

I had to help save myself.

Found

At night when the moon is high, and the lights are blazing from the

nightlight,

I sit and watch you breathe.

You snore like a freight train, like someone in a movie,

Like all you're missing is a long sleep cap hood and a long white sleep shirt

and a candle nearby burning down to nubs.

At night tucked next to you,

I slip my fingers beneath your hair and smooth my hands along your back,

Willing you to only dream of sweet things.

I push your hair out of your eyes and adjust your blanket for you,

Lay my head back down on my pillow next to yours,

And marvel your beauty.

I've never seen someone so beautiful.

I say it all the time, but I don't think you believe me.

Your strong brow and nose tucked next to the kindest eyes I've ever seen.

Lucious locks of hair tumbling down like a crown over you

Your mane is glorious

My little lion boy.

You rattle your breaths in and out.

I thought I would hate that

Get no sleep

Resent you when the morning comes to yank the blinds open,

But instead, I like it

I like to watch you dream

Green eyes closed

Your heart thumping away,

The white noise of your sleep lulls me into mine.

Your arms find me always.

Pull me tight against you.

Sheets shoved away from your chest.

Dead asleep

But still, you find me.

I'm never lost when I'm with you.

Family Heirloom

The way we curl inside ourselves in the winter.

The sun goes away and so do we.

The way we cry and cry and can't stop.

Eating just enough to get by,

Everything sounds gross again.

We yearn and look out the window and fill bathtubs full of teardrops.

This ache was handed down by my mother,

And her mother before her,

And hers before.

We all carry this sadness.

It's stitched into us

From the womb.

Kindred Spirits

And she was a child

And I was a child

Here by the sea

And our love

Oh, our love,

Hollowed me out

When I watched my love for you forsake me.

Your Everest

Maybe I'm like a mountain.

Looked at like a challenge to be conquered

Acquiesced under someone else.

Is that how you view me?

As something to win?

Kitchen Stool

I sit under the warm kitchen lights

Stirring a pot on the stove.

It's late,

Later than reasonable.

I pick up the phone anyway.

Call you,

Picture a thread connecting us through telephone lines when you pick up.

Far away

Yet stitching us up tight and close.

My Hiraeth

That will always be my Hiraeth.

My longing for a home that never was or never will be.

I feel the waves inside me lapping against the shore,

Beating the same rhythm.

They want to go home.

"We have no home,"

I gently whisper back,

Lulling them back to sleep.

Laser Tattoo Removal

For years I searched for grace and peace through religion

And kept bumping up against the hate I found inside church walls.

I sit through tattoo removal sessions now.

The laser eating the ink in my skin,

The cross slowly fading.

I find my grace elsewhere now.

Marshmallow Girlhood Soft and Light

As I grew my sweet tooth did too,

Ripped into countless bags of caramels,

Pastries were my breakfast,

Licorice for lunch.

Anything with a cream puff was what would get me through the next hour,

Sweeten me up,

Soften the taste of pennies in my mouth.

You must swallow a certain amount as a woman,

Most of it disgusting.

Trust me that a rose macaron helps it slide down easier,

Keeps you sugared.

Docile.

Inkwells Full of The Stuff

My heart was so heavy I wondered how it kept beating.

One day I finally twisted it to wring it out

But inside wasn't blood,

It was just blue pen ink.

Over the years

I wrote pages and pages and pages,

Until the ink must have entered my veins,

Dripped from my wounds,

Spilled from my mouth.

Now it keeps my inkwells full.

Don't Trust the Water Here

We never drank the water at my grandmother's house.

It stank of iron,

Tinged everything it touched with the rot of orange fog.

We learned never to drink from the water hose,

The sink,

Or the fridge.

It wasn't worth it in the end.

The stench of death would cling to you for far longer than you were thirsty.

Still or Sparkling?

The first time I saw you cry you laughed first.

Shock leaving your lips,

Sobs choked from your throat,

Your crown dirty and matted on your head,

Chest covered in blood,

Fingers swollen.

I watched your eyes roll back in your head

Whites flashing,

Grimace across your face.

But all I could do was offer you a sip of water

While I watched you drown.

Fairy Godmothers and Snakes

Once upon a time in a high tower I was locked up tight

And my nurse came in the middle of the night.

She showed me her teeth and watched me squirm,

Proclaimed I didn't need pain meds,

Though her eyes were hungry when she said it.

I watched her watching me,

Savoring my pain on her tongue.

When I cried out, she just tutted,

Told me I was okay,

I didn't need the help.

Forked tongue flashed as she licked her lips.

So, I watched the moon rise and fall

And the sun begin to creep up to take its place.

I watched her gleeful back retreating with the stars.

My cheeks dry and hot,

Eyes cracked and streaming,

Exhausted chest heaving,

A labor for every breath.

But finally, with the sunrise, a fairy godmother came to my aid.

Tipping potion bottles into my mouth,

Soothing me back to sleep,

To a land of nightmares,

Needles piercing my skin,

Of exhaustion so deep I stopped feeling the pain,

Dreamt only of snakes with hungry eyes.

Pricked Her Finger

Once upon a time,

I boarded a vessel across the sea

To a new kingdom.

The air was full of magic,

The sky of glittering stone and steel,

Boulangeries on every corner,

Fresh flowers along the cobbled side streets.

I lived in a teeny tiny garret high among the clouds.

It was only 97 square feet

But I made it home.

I scrubbed the walls and the floors,

Hung each inch with art and left no room for the walls to breathe.

The sky sparkled every night outside my window,

A show for one.

The rooftops around me glistened with glamorous women smoking from

their balconies.

I would spend hours just staring down my street below.

Every day I descended the iron stairs into the belly of Paris

And trains swirled me across the arrondissements.

I bumped along through crowds of people,

Did my shopping quickly and quietly,

And never once remembered to smile.

This princess befell a curse,

Where I fell deep deep asleep

And could not remember how to open my eyes

And when I woke up it all felt like a dream.

I was again in my own kingdom.

Glitter skies long gone.

All I kept was the curse

And the sparkles in my eyes.

Lifeboat in a Tsunami

Panic works its icy hot fingers down underneath my skull,

Playing tricks on me.

Digging into my bones,

Nestling into my skin.

I watch you scream.

Your skin is full of tubes and wires and my eyes are dead now.

We never stood a chance.

This place was always dangerous.

We just forgot.

Oily hatred pours out from the marrow of my bones.

My hand finds yours in the darkness again and again.

The only lifeboat in the sea,

We are tossed about this storm.

We are sinking.

At least we are together even at the end.

I Never Learn

I water my plants in the rain.

I never know when to leave well enough alone.

Cursed and Beloved

Moss blooms beneath my head.

Hair splayed out and wild on my pillowcase

The waste already one with the fabric.

The lush green emanates from my fingertips.

Whatever I brush against starts sprouting seedlings of decay.

Luscious death flowers and preens pretty for an audience

While it infects everything around it.

I am the harbinger of bad luck,

Of infection,

Of rot.

Everything I touch spoils.

Oh. Do You Sing?

Music used to be the secret I hugged right to my chest.

My laugh was in thirds.

Notes slipping between my teeth,

Diaphragm extended,

Breathing from the root of me,

Cleaved in half by breaths as big as the sea.

Making sure my smile was on, my soft palate was lifted, my sternum raised,

my shoulders back and relaxed,

My throat perfectly poised in the best angle to let sound leave me.

My feet perfectly turned,

My legs hip width apart.

Don't lock your knees,

Breathe from your knees,

No, breathe from your vagina,

No, breathe from your feet.

Okay, breathe better.

Oh, that was too many breaths.

Make them last.

Stretch them.

Don't let your chest collapse.

No, think of it as breathing in the round,

Of breathing like a balloon,

Of breathing like you're underwater.

If you can't breathe out peanut butter that's stuck in your throat, you're not even a singer.

If you consume dairy do you even care?

You call yourself a musician but really how many instruments can you sight read at the drop of a hat?

You think you're a professional?

Professionals are willing to be broken down to their cores for this,

Beaten to their worst for this,

To beg for this and thank them for it.

If you really wanted it, you would take the unpaid internships,

But you would also figure out how to afford the ten grand summer programs.

You'll work for free

Until you're good enough to get paid.

You'll suffer and you'll like it.

No, you'll crave it

Cry out for it.

Plead for an opportunity to be in the rooms where things happen.

But silly girl, they already decided you're rejected the moment they saw you.

The spread of your hips too wide.

Thank you for your time.

If you wanted this bad enough, you would be willing to give them

everything.

To chisel yourself down

Mentally and physically,

Until you were only what they wanted,

Everything else sloughed off like a sweater in April.

A true singer sings to the back of the house.

A true singer can hit a high C in a corset sitting on the floor,

Boning impaling her.

I stopped singing.

So, I only scream now.

But don't worry,

My vibrato is still perfect.

Please Don't Bite Me

There's no such thing as a free lunch they jeer.

I shake my head lightly,

Pouring wine down your throat,

Dabbing at the thin line dripping from your lips.

There is a free lunch

When it is a gift

From people you love

Who just want you to eat.

Now I Take Hydroxyzine

My hands won't let me cook you dinner.

They shake.

When the recipe says chop the veggies I shake like a leaf

Overwhelmed in the fact I know it won't be perfect,

Already defeated at the final product that doesn't even exist.

My hands won't let me write you a letter.

They shake.

The words already inadequate

Before they even meet the paper

And if they're not worthy why waste the stamp?

So I don't write letters anymore.

My mouth doesn't open when I need you.

The words click against the back of my teeth,

Throat completely closes,

Tears cloud my eyes.

My need will come across as too big, too loud, too scared, too ugly.

So I swallow and quietly wait for it to pass,

My hands shaking,

The words never making it past my lips.

Theatre Lights

When the lights at the movie came up

I turned and caught your eye.

In shock you asked if it was me

And hugged me quick before running to your car through the snow flurries.

Our lockers were next to each other sixth to eighth grade,

Your name directly above mine in the alphabet.

You saw me.

You saw me in a theatre when the lights came up

Just like you saw me before I knew how to put on makeup.

This woman saw me for years before I knew anything at all.

Before I knew how not to bleed through every pair of pants I owned,

How to brush my hair correctly,

How to be a woman,

And you recognized me today.

Even with the hair done,

Lipstick slicked on,

Eyes made up,

Long coat and gloves on,

You saw me.

Thanks.

Hover D'oeuvres

So, eat me,

Bones and all.

Relish me in chomping bites

Or maybe whole,

Pulling my spine out like a kebab.

Pluck me limb from limb

And smack your lips when you're done,

Because you only ever viewed me as something to be devoured.

Music School Anxieties

Some things never leave us.

I sleep with my baby blanket over my throat,

An old singing habit as hard to shake as nicotine.

Sap Melts in Spring

Sadness is sticky.

It seeps into every crack in my heart and weighs it down

Until I feel like I'm sinking to the bottom of the ocean,

Never to see the stars again.

Sadness is sticky.

I feel it hardening me,

Body becoming heavier,

Stuck in place.

Sadness is sticky.

I watch it keep people months,

Years,

Decades.

And I slowly start trying to scrape layers off,

Thawing with the weather,

Scared to be stuck here too.

Nightlights

Late at night, I miss sharing a room with my sister.

Hearing her breathing a handsbreadth away,

Nightlight shining on the ceiling,

Stuffed animals piled in next to us.

Now I just cry in the shower

And ask myself

Can't I knock it off already?

Isn't this sort of played out?

Embarrassed to have caused such a scene I gulp back the tears,

Scratch my skin raw under the boiling water,

Towel myself off with scathing glances,

Pinching my thighs with pricks of hatred.

Toss back a few pills to numb myself out

Before tucking myself in next to my nightmares,

A warm glass of regret on the nightstand.

No nightlights allowed here.

Mold

Whenever I open my lips mold flutters out

Like dandelion puffs.

It thrusts out of my throat and chokes the air near me.

There's nothing really left to say though, is there?

Maybe this is already too much.

Epilogue

So it's sun-soaked days of Shakespeare in the park.

Fizzy waters and jams and soft cheese spread on toast.

Butterflies and sunbeams and watching the sky change across hours.

This is what it's like to hold on,

To beat the darkness,

To find the dawn.

EULOGY

When you feel your dreams rotting underneath your palms

Pulpy and mashed,

Beetles scuttling,

Maggots feasting--

Maybe that's when you know to walk away.

I didn't dream of it a moment before

I held on, way past rigor mortis,

Well into decay.

Fairytale Cottage

Now I live in a little home,

Full of fresh flowers,

Hung with red velvet curtains on golden rods

That tumble to the carpets we lovingly put down.

Our desks sit side by side beneath the window facing the bird feeder

And our dining table is the one my grandparents sat at together.

We cook meals

And laugh when it goes badly.

No one ever slams the cupboard doors

And no one puts the milk away with anger.

He kisses me and feeds me a bite of chocolate while I stir the gently

bubbling sauce at the stove.

We snuggle beneath mountains of blankets

And watch movies together on the couch,

Our baby tucked between us,

The rain coming down outside.

These are the moments I dreamed of.

These are the ones I held on for.

This has happiness.

This is love.

THE END

Love Notes

To every single person who read this or my debut book and had my words enter their world— thank you endlessly. It is still shocking and an honor of my life to have been able to share my heart with you.

This would have never been possible without my team of editors: Rachel Carpenter, Meg Rojahn, Christen Wegener, Anna Nelson, and Riley Cerda.

This amazing cover was brought to life by the endlessly kind Ash Nicole Gill who is so talented it is unreal.

To my family and loved ones who have been so proud of me and helped me peddle around my book the last few years, especially my mom who told me I was a writer since I was five and never let me forget it. Thank you. Love you.

Jordan Parker Holmes who helped me when things felt too dark and literally came into my home and sat with me when it all felt too hard. Matthew Z Gillin who is never far, as we are fellow Terrors™ and we stick together forever. Through thick and thin, I know we have each other.

Lizzy Anderson for being the most precious angel on earth. Thank you for all of it always and forever.

Finally, to my loves, my little gentlemen, who are woven into these pages in snippets and sections, who came into my life and changed it all for the better. I love you.

VICTORIA LAUREN was raised on a steady diet of fairy tales and love songs.

She studied opera performance as a dramatic coloratura soprano and cites music as her first love and books as her lifelong affair. She loves travel, collects way too many kitschy antiques, and lives in the Midwest with the love of her life, Nick, and their baby.

Promises of Poison is her second book.

www.ingramcontent.com/pod-product-compliance
Lightning Source LLC
Chambersburg PA
CBHW082251120626
46553CB00014B/2798